RECORDED VERSIONS
GUITAR

AUTHENTIC TRANSCRIPTIONS
WITH NOTES AND TABLATURE

Transcribed By
STEVE GORENBERG
and
KERRY O'BRIEN

R.E.M.
AUTOMATIC FOR THE PEOPLE

R.E.M.

All photos by Anton Corbijn.

HAL•LEONARD
CORPORATION

7777 W. BLUEMOUND RD. P.O. BOX 13819 MILWAUKEE, WI 53213

Drive

Words and Music by
Bill Berry, Peter Buck,
Mike Mills and Michael Stipe

Try Not To Breathe

Words and Music by
Bill Berry, Peter Buck, Mike Mills and Michael Stipe

Moderately ♩. = 66

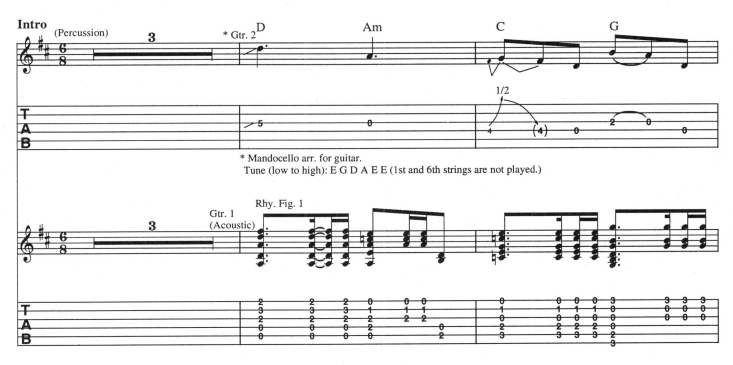

* Mandocello arr. for guitar.
Tune (low to high): E G D A E E (1st and 6th strings are not played.)

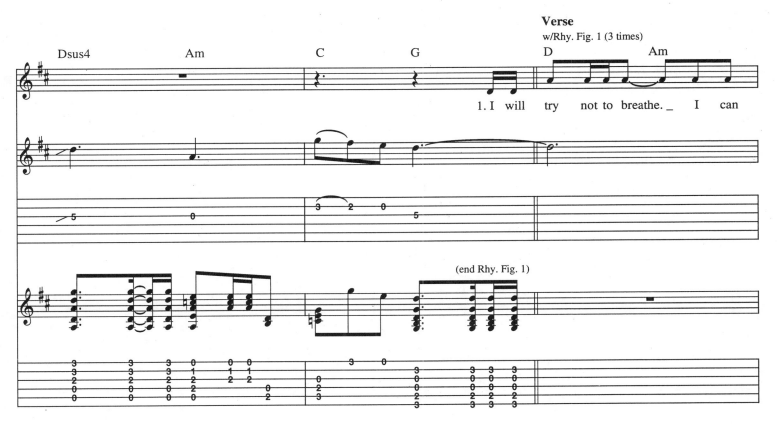

hold my head still with my hands at my knees. __ These eyes are the eyes __ of the

old, shiv - er and fold. _____ I will

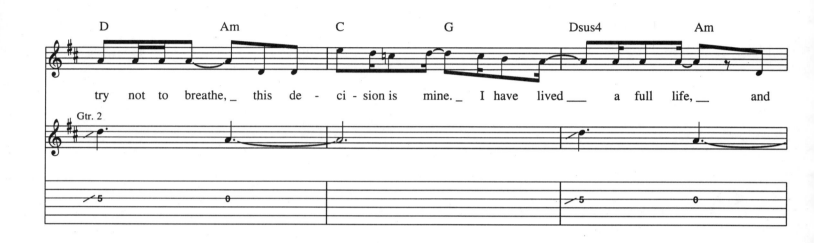

try not to breathe, _ this de - ci - sion is mine. I have lived ___ a full life, __ and

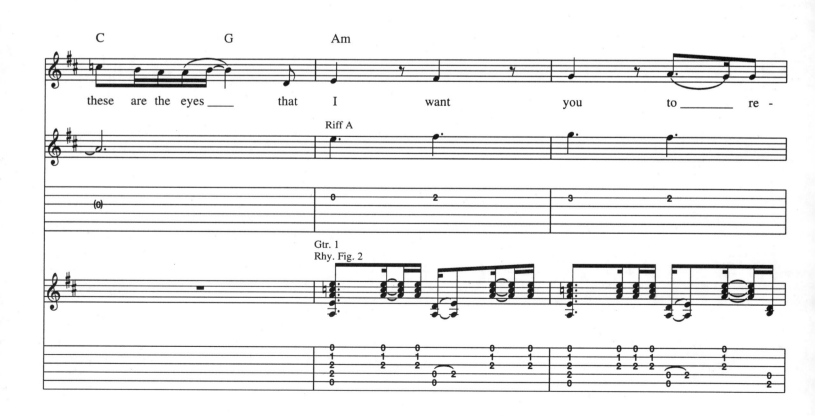

these are the eyes ____ that I want you to _____ re -

til all these shiv- ers ___ sub- side. ___   Just look in ___ my

eyes. ___   I will try not to wor- ry you.

*2nd time bass and drums tacet (next 8 bars).

I have seen things _ that you will _____ nev- er see. ___   Leave it to mem- o- ry me. _

1. I shud- der ___ to breathe. _
2. Don't dare me ___ to breathe. _

Chorus
w/Rhy. Fig. 2 & Riff A

I   want   you   to _____ re- mem - ber. _____

Gtr. 3
(Acoustic)

You will nev- er ___ see.

Oh.   (cont. in Fill 1)

13

Bridge

w/Rhy. Fig. 5

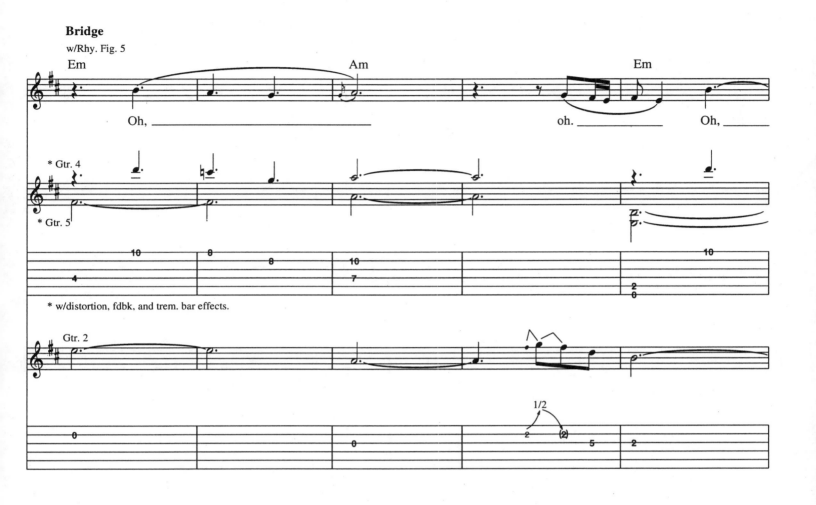

* w/distortion, fdbk, and trem. bar effects.

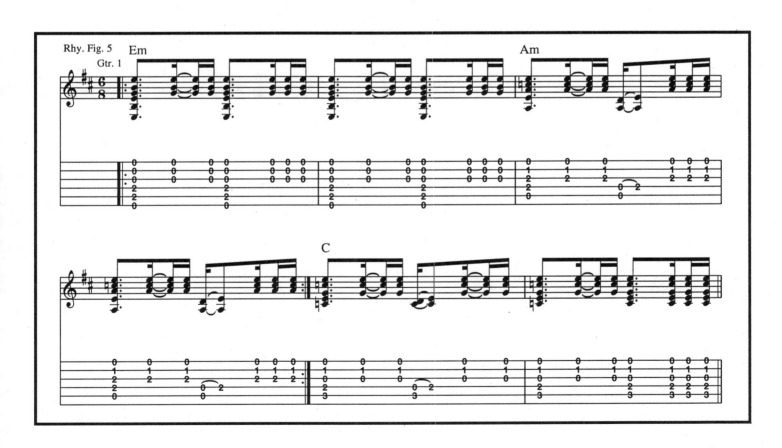

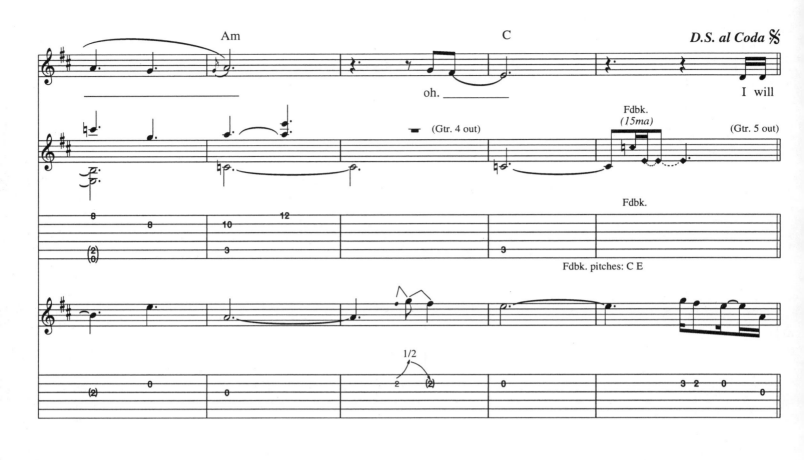

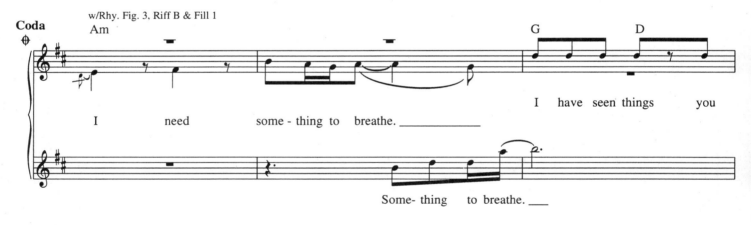

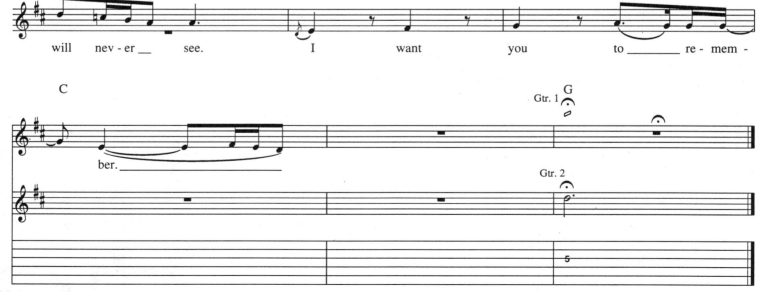

The Sidewinder Sleeps Tonite

Words and Music by Bill Berry, Peter Buck, Mike Mills and Michael Stipe

Everybody Hurts

Words and Music by
Bill Berry, Peter Buck,
Mike Mills and Michael Stipe

ev - ery - bod- y cries. ___

And

ev - ery - bod-y hurts ___   some -

(end Rhy. Fig. 2A)
(end Rhy. Fig. 2)

w/Rhy. Fig. 1 (2 times)

times. _____

Some - times ev - ery- thing is   wrong.

28

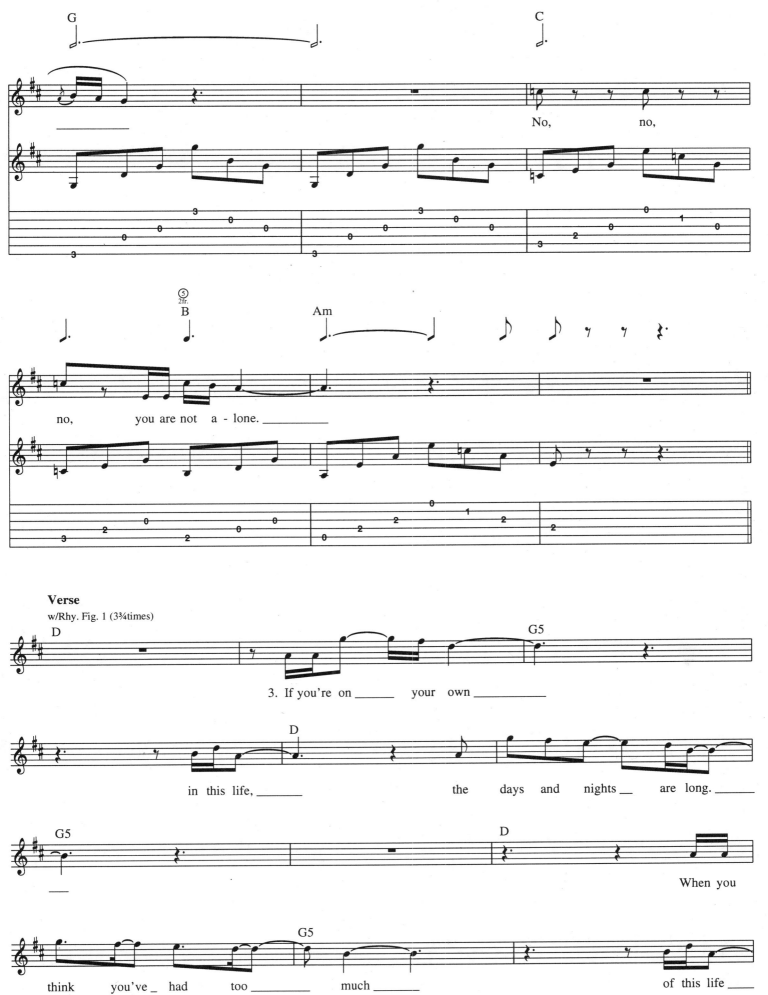

*Band tacet this measure.

Outro

Repeat and fade

New Orleans Instrumental No. 1

Words and Music by Bill Berry, Peter Buck, Mike Mills and Michael Stipe

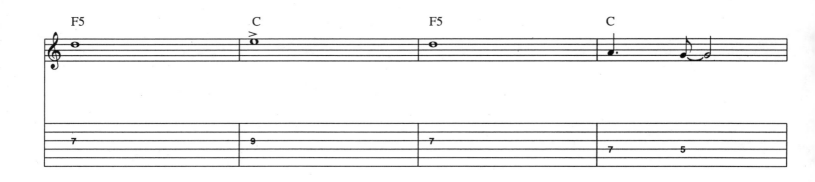

Begin fade

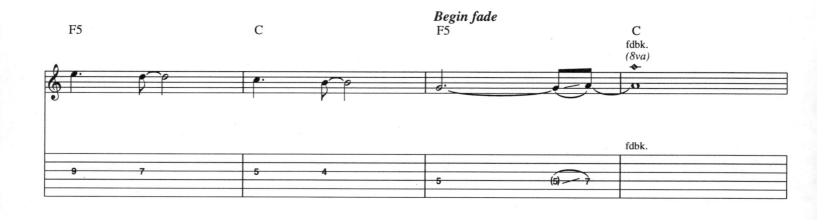

Fade out

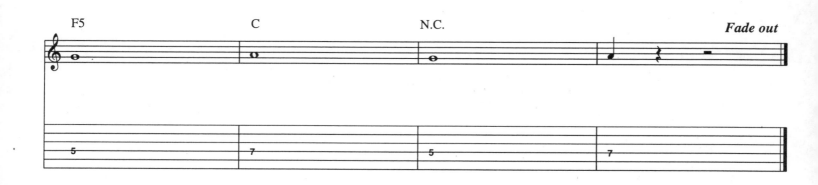

Sweetness Follows

Words and Music by Bill Berry, Peter Buck, Mike Mills and Michael Stipe

Dis - tanced from one, ___ blind to the ___ oth - er.

(end Rhy. Fig. 2)

w/Rhy. Fig. 2

Lis - ten here, my sis - ter and my ___ broth - er.

What would you care if you ___ lost the ___ oth - er? I al - ways won - der why

did we ___ both - er? Dis - tanced from one, ___ deaf to the ___ oth - er.

Chorus
w/Riff B
G6   A6sus2   G6   A6sus2

w/Rhy. Fig. 1 & Riff A
E5

Oh, _____ oh, _____ but sweet - ness fol - lows. ___

Rhy. Fig. 3   (end Rhy. Fig. 3)

Riff B
Gtr. 2

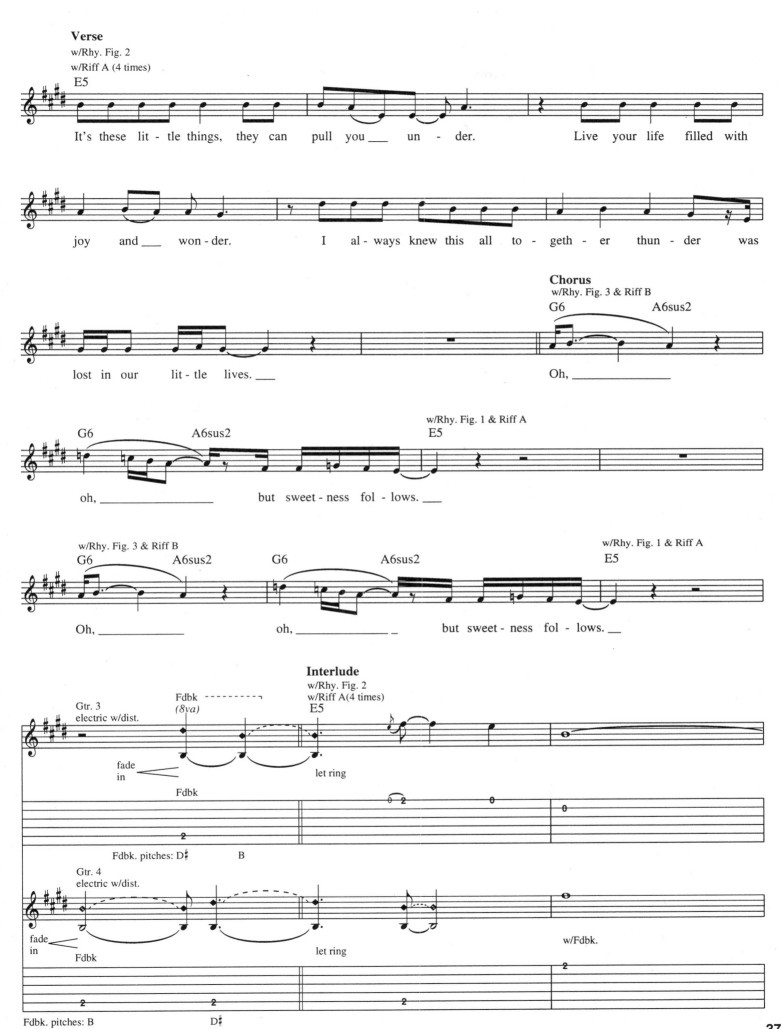

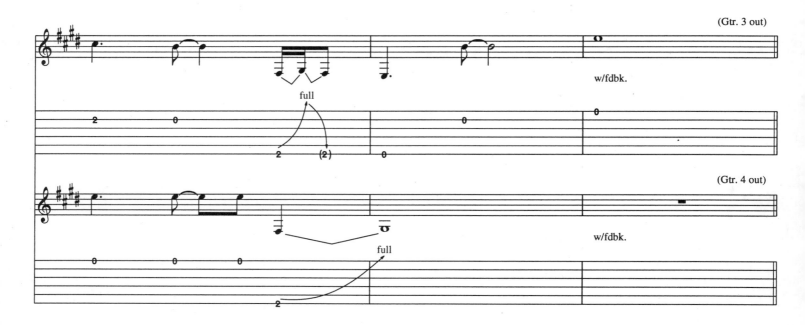

Verse
w/Rhy. Fig. 2
w/Riff A (4 times)

It's these lit - tle things, that can pull you ___ un - der. Live your life filled with

joy and ___ thun - der. Yeah, yeah, we were al - to - geth - er

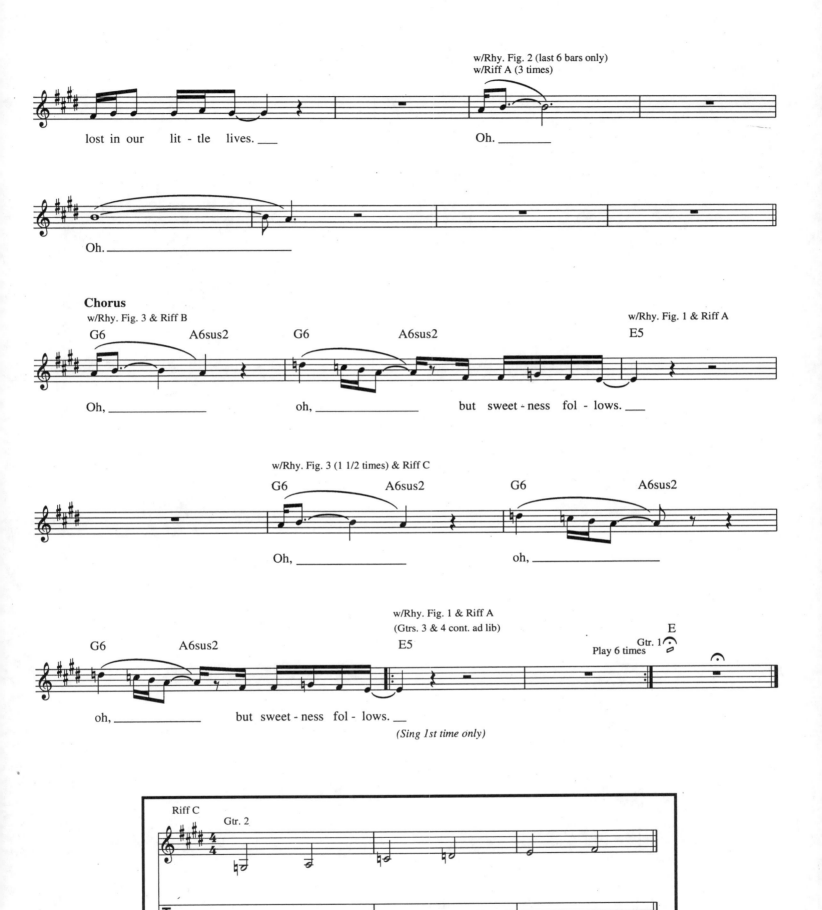

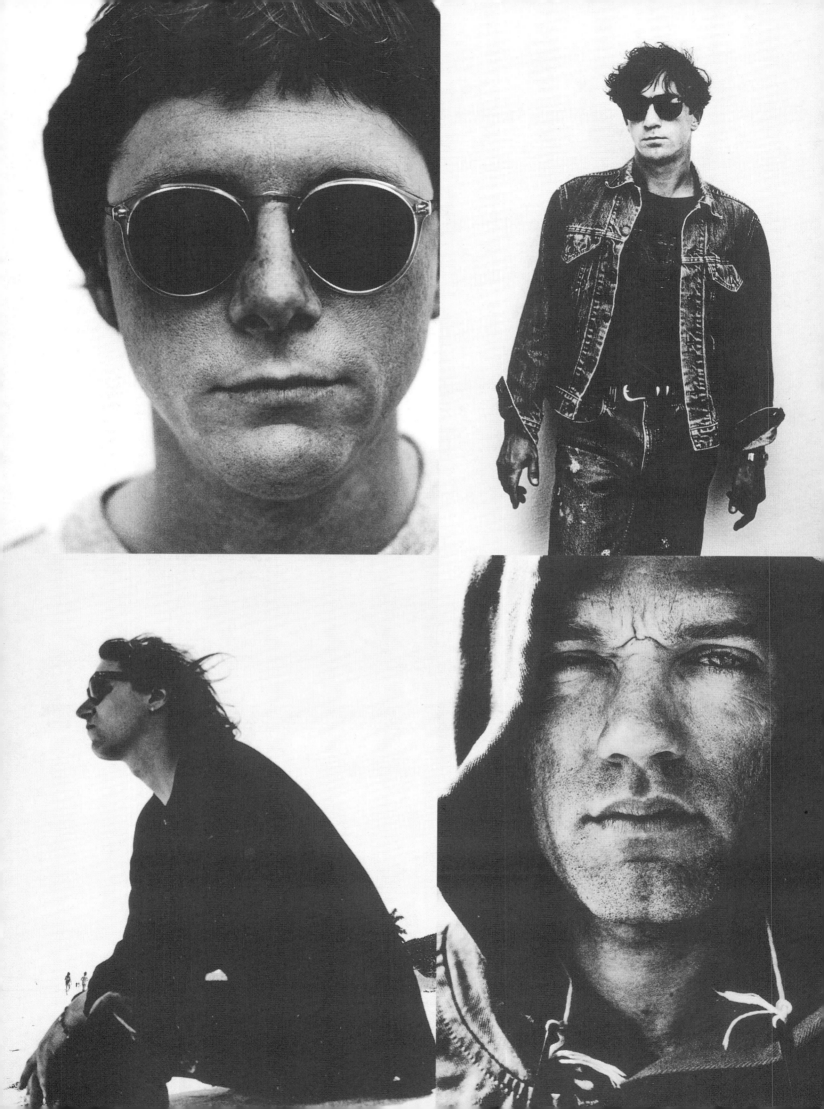

Monty Got A Raw Deal

Words and Music by Bill Berry, Peter Buck, Mike Mills and Michael Stipe

Bm   Aadd9   E5   Em
he - roes don't _ come eas - y.   Now, non - sense is - n't new _

G   Em   G
_ ` to me. ___   I know my head, __ I know __ my feet. __   But

Em   G   Bm   Aadd9
mis - chief knocked _ me in _____ the knees, __ said just let go. __

E5   w/Rhy. Fill 1   Bm   Aadd9   E5
_   Just let go. _____   2. I

Verse
w/Riff A (3 times)   (end Rhy. Fig. 2)   w/Rhy. Fig. 2 (2 times)
Em   Emsus4 Em   G   Gsus2   G   Em   Emsus4 Em
Rhy. Fig. 2
saw the o - cean meet ___ the man. __   I saw you bur - ied in _
(3.) non - sense does - n't mean ___ a thing. __   They tried to bust you in _

G   Gsus2   G   Em   Emsus4 Em   G   Gsus2   G
_ the sand. __   A friend was there __ to hold ____ your hand, __ said
_ a sting. __   But vir - tue is - n't ev - ery - thing. __ So

Rhy. Fill 1   Em

Riff A (Gtr. 2)
* Gtr. 2

* Mandolin arr. for gtr. (capo 3rd fret)

Ignoreland

Words and Music by
Bill Berry, Peter Buck,
Mike Mills and Michael Stipe

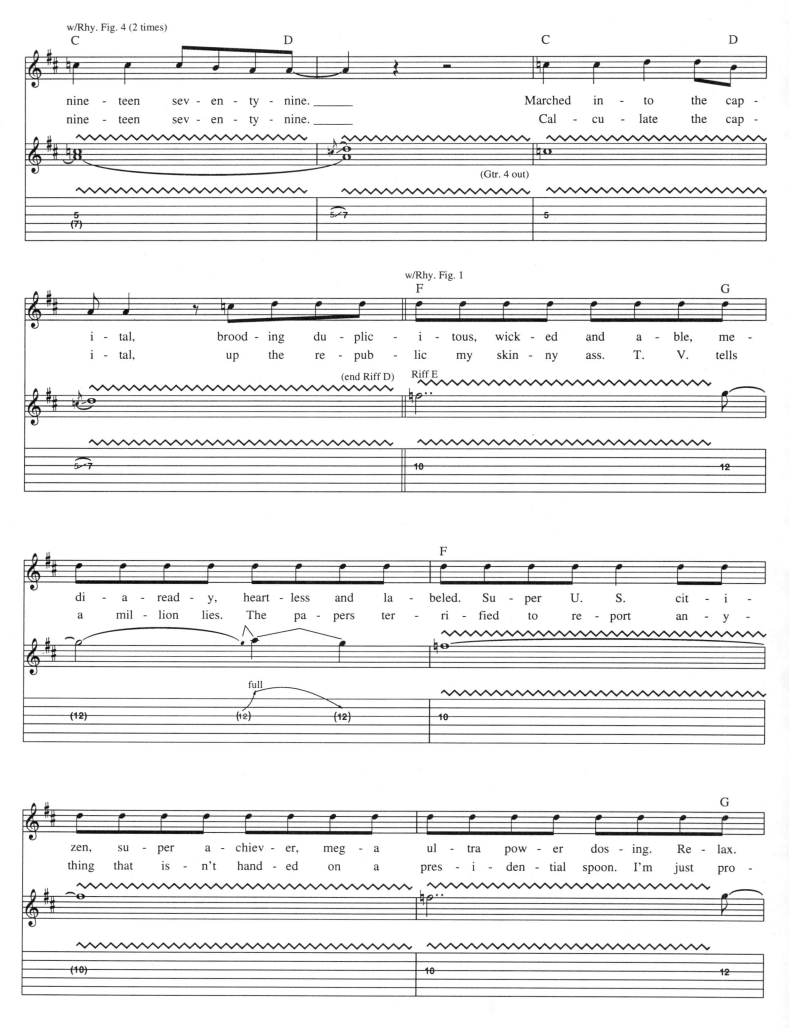

Chorus
*w/Rhy. Fig. 2 and Riffs A & B

*2nd time play 1st 6 bars only
(Rhy. Fig. 2 and Riffs A & B).

Bridge

all the same. ___   Some-one's got to take ___ the blame. ___   I

Verse
w/Rhy. Fig. 3 (2 times)

D5   D7(no 3rd)   w/Riff C
                                         G/D

know that this is vit - ri - ol. ___   No so - lu - tion,

Em7   D5   D7(no 3rd)

spleen vent - ing. But I _____ feel bet - ter hav - ing screamed; _don't

G/D   Em7   w/Rhy. Fig. 4 (3 times) and Riff D
                                               C   D

you? _____   They des - e - crated _ win -

                                 C   D

ter,   nine - teen sev - en - ty - nine. ____

C   D

Cap - i - tal col - lat - er - al.   Brood - ing du - plic -

w/Rhy. Fig. 1 and Riff E
F   G

i - tous, wick - ed and a - ble, me - di - a - read - y, heart - less and la -

beled. Su - per U. S. cit - i - zen, su - per a - chiev - er, meg - a

ul - tra pow - er dos - ing. Re - lax. De - fense, de - fense, de - fense, de - fense.

Chorus
w/Rhy. Fig. 2 and Riffs A & B (all 1st 4 bars only, 2 times)

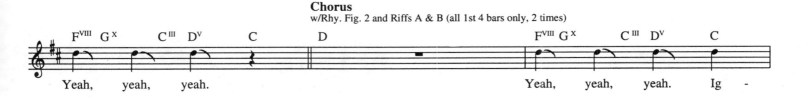

Yeah, yeah, yeah. Yeah, yeah, yeah. Ig -

nore - land. __ Yeah, yeah, yeah. Ig - nore - land. __

Yeah, yeah, yeah. Ig - nore - land. __ Yeah, yeah, yeah.

Outro
w/Rhy. Fig. 2 and Riffs A & B (all 1st 6 bars only)

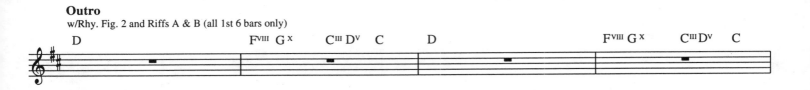

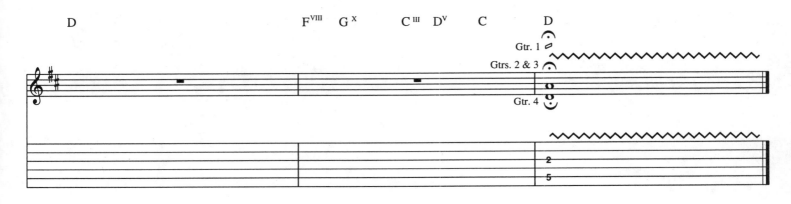

Star Me Kitten

Words and Music by Bill Berry, Peter Buck, Mike Mills and Michael Stipe

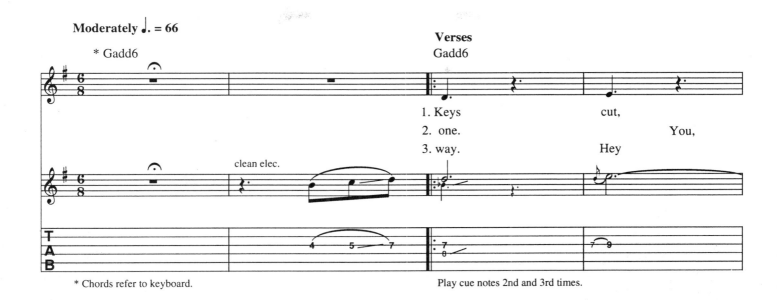

* Chords refer to keyboard.

Play cue notes 2nd and 3rd times.

for   a   life - times   use.   I've   changed   the   locks   and

hear,   I   hear   them   screech - ing   through   the   door

love   is   tired.   I've   changed   the   locks.   Have

Bridge

you   can't   have

from   our   drive -

I   mis - placed   you?

Have   we   lost _____ our _____ minds? _

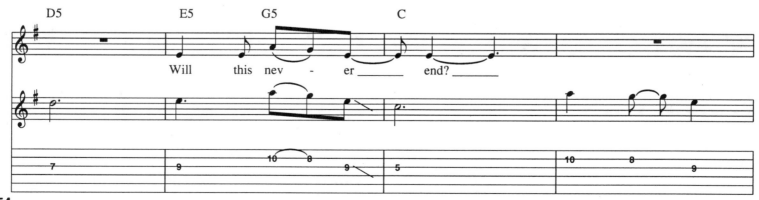

Will   this   nev - er _____ end? _____

54

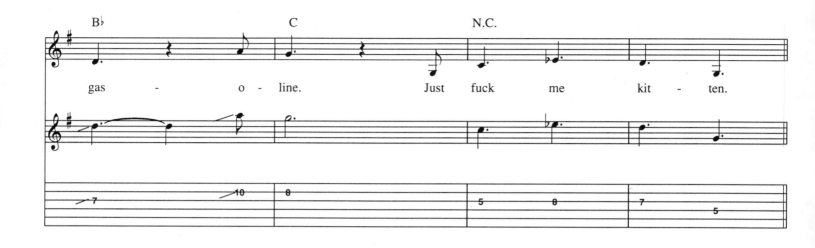

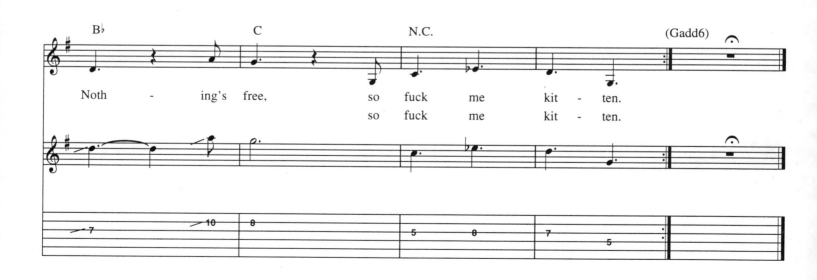

Man On The Moon

Words and Music by Bill Berry, Peter Buck, Mike Mills and Michael Stipe

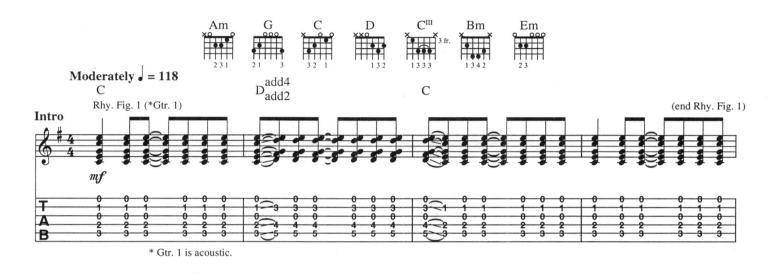

* Gtr. 1 is acoustic.

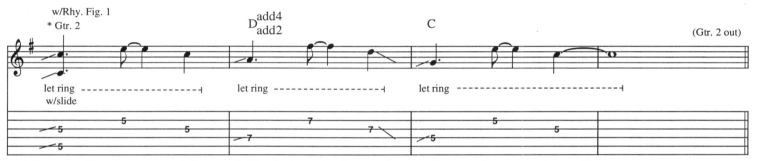

* Gtr. 2 tunes 5th string down one whole step to G. 6th string is not played and may be removed or tuned down one whole step to D.

Verse

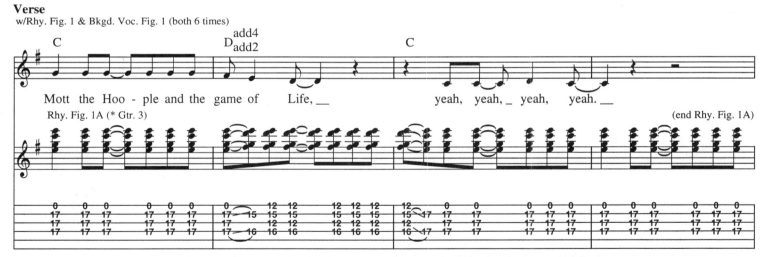

Mott the Hoo - ple and the game of Life, __ yeah, yeah, _ yeah, yeah. __

* Gtr. 3 is mandolin arr. for gtr. In order to simulate open strings found on the mandolin, Gtr. 3 should be played w/capo at 12th fret.

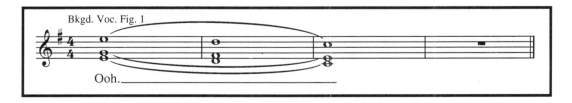

Ooh. ___

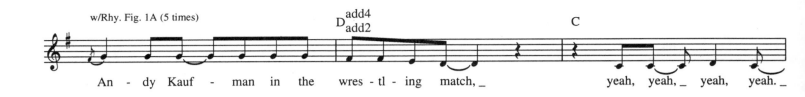

w/Rhy. Fig. 1A (5 times)

D add4 add2   C

An - dy Kauf - man in the wres - tl - ing match, _ yeah, yeah, _ yeah, yeah.

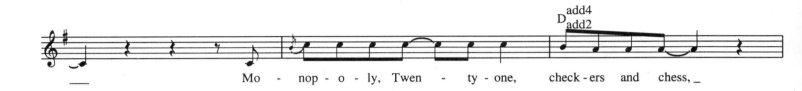

D add4 add2

_ Mo - nop - o - ly, Twen - ty - one, check - ers and chess, _

C

yeah, yeah, _ yeah, yeah. _ Mis - ter Fred Blas - sie in a

D add4 add2   C

break - fast mess, _ yeah, yeah, _ yeah, yeah. _

w/Rhy. Fig. 1B (2 times)

D add4 add2   C

Let's play Twist - er, let's _ play Risk, _ yeah, yeah, _ yeah, yeah. _ I'll

D add4 add2   C

see you in heav - en if you make the list, _ yeah, yeah, _ yeah, yeah. _ Now

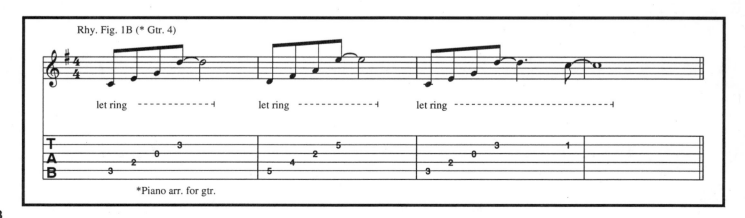

Rhy. Fig. 1B (* Gtr. 4)

let ring   let ring   let ring

*Piano arr. for gtr.

Pre-chorus

An- dy, did you hear a - bout this one? Tell me are you locked in the punch? _ Hey

An -dy, are you goof-ing on El - vis? Hey ba- by, are we los -ing touch? _

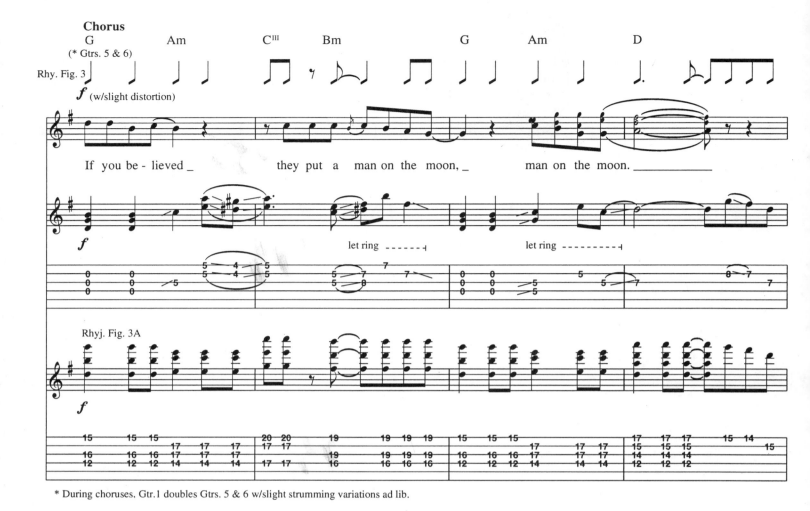

* During choruses, Gtr.1 doubles Gtrs. 5 & 6 w/slight strumming variations ad lib.

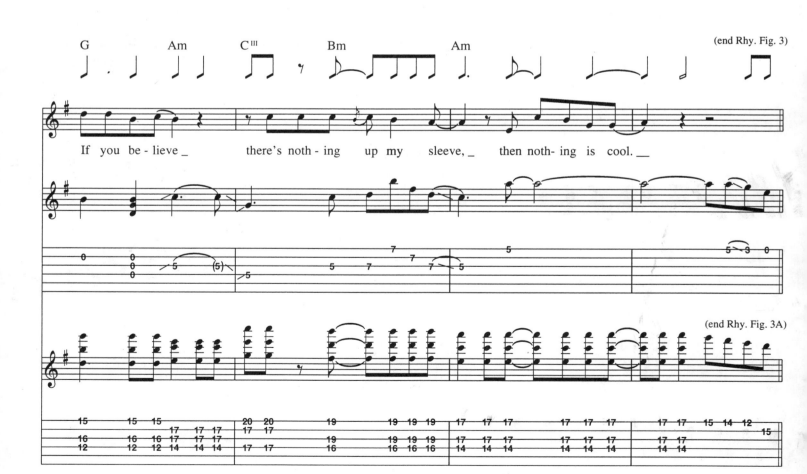

Verse
w/Rhy. Figs. 1 & 1A & Bkgd. Voc. Fig. 1 (all 4 times)

Mos- es went walk- ing with the staff of wood, _ yeah, yeah, _ yeah, yeah. _

New- ton got beaned by the ap- ple good, _ yeah, yeah, _ yeah, yeah. _

w/Rhy. Fig. 1B (2 times)

E - gypt was trou - bled by the hor - ri - ble asp, __ yeah, yeah, _ yeah, yeah. _

Mis - ter Charles Dar- win had the gall to ask, _ yeah, yeah, _ yeah, yeah. _ Now

Nightswimming

Words and Music by Bill Berry, Peter Buck, Mike Mills and Michael Stipe

turned a - round back - wards so the wind - shield shows. _

Ev - er - y street - light re - veals ___ the pic - ture in ___ re - verse. _

Still, it's so ___ much clear - er.

I for - got ___ my shirt ___ at ___ the wa - ter's edge. _____ The

moon is low ___ to - night. ____

w/Rhy. Fig. 1

Verse

w/Rhy. Fig. 2 (8 times)

2. Night - swim - ming de - serves ___ a qui - et night. _____

___ I'm not sure all these peo - ple un - der - stand. _

___ It's not like years ___ a - go, _____ the

ev - ery street - light a ____ re - mind - er.   Night - swim -

ming   de - serves a qui - et   night, ___

de - serves a qui - et   night. ___

Outro
w/Rhy. Fig. 2 (2 times)

Find The River

Words and Music by Bill Berry, Peter Buck, Mike Mills and Michael Stipe

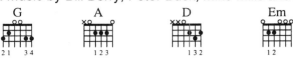

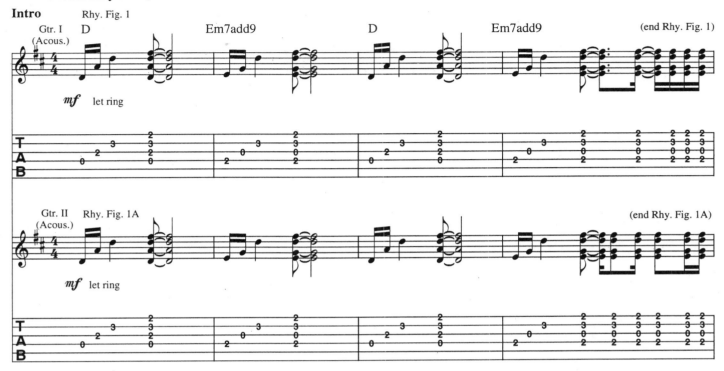

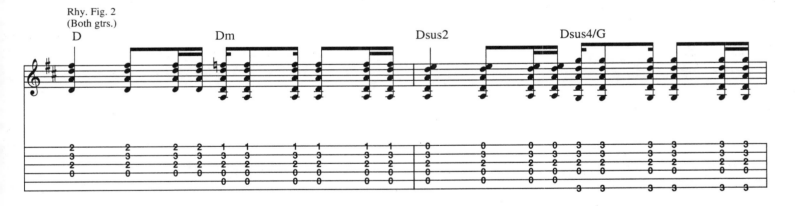

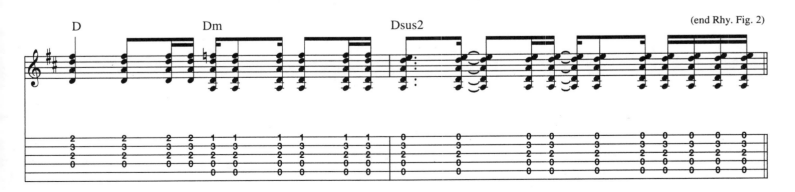

ger, lem - on, in - di - go, co - ri - an - der stem _ and rose _ of hay. __

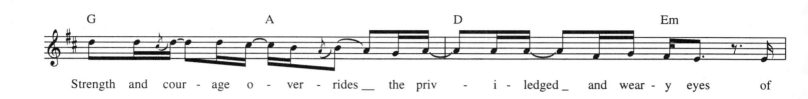

Strength and cour - age o - ver - rides __ the priv - i - ledged _ and wear - y eyes of

w/Rhy. Fig. 3 (1st 3 bars only)

riv - er po - et search _ na - iv - e - te. __ Pick up here __ and chase _ the ride, _ the

riv - er emp - ties to the tide. All of this __ is com - ing your ____ way. _

NOTATION LEGEND

RECORDED VERSIONS
The Best Note-For-Note Transcriptions Available

GUITAR — RECORDED VERSIONS

ALL BOOKS INCLUDE TABLATURE

00694909	Aerosmith – Get A Grip $19.95
00692015	Aerosmith's Greatest Hits $18.95
00660133	Aerosmith – Pump $18.95
00694865	Alice In Chains – Dirt................................$18.95
00660225	Alice In Chains – Facelift...........................$18.95
00694826	Anthrax – Attack Of The Killer B's $18.95
00660227	Anthrax – Persistence Of Time $18.95
00694797	Armored Saint – Symbol Of Salvation $18.95
00694876	Chet Atkins – Contemporary Styles $18.95
00660051	Badlands $18.95
00694880	Beatles – Abbey Road.................................$18.95
00694832	Beatles For Acoustic Guitar $18.95
00660140	Beatles Guitar Book....................................$18.95
00694891	Beatles – Revolver......................................$18.95
00694863	Beatles – Sgt. Pepper's Lonely Hearts Club Band $18.95
00694884	The Best of George Benson $19.95
00692385	Chuck Berry $18.95
00692200	Black Sabbath – We Sold Our Soul For Rock 'N' Roll $18.95
00694821	Blue Heaven – Great Blues Guitar $18.95
00694770	Jon Bon Jovi – Blaze Of Glory..................$18.95
00694871	Bon Jovi – Keep The Faith $18.95
00694774	Bon Jovi – New Jersey...............................$18.95
00694775	Bon Jovi – Slippery When Wet...................$18.95
00694762	Cinderella – Heartbreak Station $18.95
00692376	Cinderella – Long Cold Winter $18.95
00692375	Cinderella – Night Songs...........................$18.95
00694875	Eric Clapton – Boxed Set...........................$75.00
00692392	Eric Clapton – Crossroads Vol. 1...............$22.95
00692393	Eric Clapton – Crossroads Vol. 2...............$22.95
00692394	Eric Clapton – Crossroads Vol. 3...............$22.95
00660139	Eric Clapton – Journeyman........................$18.95
00694869	Eric Clapton – Unplugged $18.95
00692391	The Best of Eric Clapton $18.95
00694896	John Mayall/Eric Clapton – Bluesbreakers ..$18.95
00694873	Eric Clapton – Timepieces $18.95
00694788	Classic Rock...$17.95
00694793	Classic Rock Instrumentals $16.95
00694837	Albert Collins – The Complete Imperial Records.............$18.95
00694862	Contemporary Country Guitar....................$18.95
00660127	Alice Cooper – Trash $18.95
00694840	Cream – Disraeli Gears $14.95
00694844	Def Leppard – Adrenalize...........................$18.95
00692440	Def Leppard – High 'N' Dry/Pyromania $18.95
00692430	Def Leppard – Hysteria..............................$18.95
00660186	Alex De Grassi Guitar Collection $16.95
00694831	Derek And The Dominos – Layla & Other Assorted Love Songs...................$19.95
00692240	Bo Diddley Guitar Solos $18.95
00660175	Dio – Lock Up The Wolves $18.95
00660178	Willie Dixon $24.95
00694915	Electric Blues Guitar Giants.......................$18.95
00694852	Electric Blues Volume 1 – Book/Cassette Pack..................................$22.95
00694800	FireHouse $18.95
00694867	FireHouse – Hold Your Fire $18.95
00694894	Frank Gambale – The Great Explorers $18.95

00694807	Danny Gatton – 88 Elmira St $17.95
00694848	Genuine Rockabilly Guitar Hits................$19.95
00660326	Guitar Heroes...$17.95
00694780	Guitar School Classics $17.95
00694768	Guitar School Greatest Hits $17.95
00694854	Buddy Guy – Damn Right, I've Got The Blues $18.95
00660325	The Harder Edge...$17.95
00694798	George Harrison Anthology $19.95
00692930	Jimi Hendrix – Are You Experienced? $19.95
00692931	Jimi Hendrix – Axis: Bold As Love $19.95
00660192	The Jimi Hendrix Concerts $24.95
00692932	Jimi Hendrix – Electric Ladyland...............$24.95
00660099	Jimi Hendrix – Radio One.........................$24.95
00660024	Jimi Hendrix – Variations On A Theme: Red House $18.95
00660029	Buddy Holly $18.95
00660200	John Lee Hooker – The Healer...................$18.95
00660169	John Lee Hooker – A Blues Legend $17.95
00694850	Iron Maiden – Fear Of The Dark...............$19.95
00694761	Iron Maiden – No Prayer For The Dying...$18.95
00693096	Iron Maiden – Power Slave/Somewhere In Time $19.95
00693095	Iron Maiden $22.95
00694833	Billy Joel For Guitar..................................$18.95
00660147	Eric Johnson Guitar Transcriptions...........$18.95
00694799	Robert Johnson – At The Crossroads.........$19.95
00693186	Judas Priest – Metal Cuts...........................$18.95
00660226	Judas Priest – Painkiller.............................$18.95
00693187	Judas Priest – Ram It Down $18.95
00693185	Judas Priest – Vintage Hits $18.95
00694764	Kentucky Headhunters – Pickin' On Nashville $18.95
00694795	Kentucky Headhunters – Electric Barnyard .$18.95
00660050	B. B. King...$18.95
00694903	The Best Of Kiss..$24.95
00660068	Kix – Blow My Fuse...................................$18.95
00694806	L.A. Guns – Hollywood Vampires $18.95
00694794	Best Of Los Lobos.....................................$18.95
00660199	The Lynch Mob – Wicked Sensation.........$18.95
00693412	Lynyrd Skynyrd..$18.95
00660174	Yngwie Malmsteen – Eclipse $18.95
00694845	Yngwie Malmsteen – Fire And Ice $18.95
00694756	Yngwie Malmsteen – Marching Out..........$18.95
00694755	Yngwie Malmsteen's Rising Force $18.95
00660001	Yngwie Malmsteen Rising Force – Odyssey..$18.95
00694757	Yngwie Malmsteen – Trilogy $18.95
00692880	Metal Madness $17.95
00694792	Metal Church – The Human Factor $18.95
00660229	Monster Metal Ballads................................$19.95
00694868	Gary Moore – After Hours $18.95
00694849	Gary Moore – The Early Years....................$18.95
00694802	Gary Moore – Still Got The Blues $18.95
00694872	Vinnie Moore – Meltdown..........................$18.95
00694895	Nirvana – Bleach..$18.95
00694913	Nirvana – In Utero $18.95
00694883	Nirvana – Nevermind $18.95
00694847	Best Of Ozzy Osbourne..............................$22.95
00694830	Ozzy Osbourne – No More Tears...............$18.95

00694855	Pearl Jam – Ten $18.9
00693800	Pink Floyd – Early Classics........................$18.9
00660188	Poison – Flesh & Blood..............................$18.9
00693865	Poison – Look What The Cat Dragged In ..$18.9
00693864	The Best Of Police $18.9
00692535	Elvis Presley $18.9
00693910	Ratt – Invasion of Your Privacy $18.9
00693911	Ratt – Out Of The Cellar $18.9
00694892	Guitar Style Of Jerry Reed.........................$18.9
00694899	REM – Automatic For The People..............$18.9
00694898	REM – Out Of Time $18.9
00660060	Robbie Robertson $18.9
00694760	Rock Classics $17.9
00693474	Rock Superstars $17.9
00694851	Rock: The 50s Volume 1 – Book/Cassette Pack..................................$19.9
00694902	Rock: The 60s Volume 1 – Book/Cassette Pack..................................$24.9
00694897	Roots Of Country Guitar $19.9
00694836	Richie Sambora – Stranger In This Town .$18.9
00694805	Scorpions – Crazy World.............................$18.9
00694870	Seattle Scene $18.9
00694885	Spin Doctors – Pocket Full Of Kryptonite .$18.9
00694796	Steelheart $18.9
00694180	Stryper – In God We Trust..........................$18.9
00694824	Best Of James Taylor $14.9
00694846	Testament – The Ritual $18.9
00694765	Testament – Souls Of Black........................$18.9
00694887	Thin Lizzy – The Best Of Thin Lizzy..........$18.9
00694410	The Best of U2...$18.9
00694411	U2 – The Joshua Tree $18.9
00694893	Unplugged – Rock Guitar's Greatest Acoustic Hits...........................$18.9
00660137	Steve Vai – Passion & Warfare $24.9
00694904	Vai – Sex and Religion $19.9
00694879	Stevie Ray Vaughan – In The Beginning....$18.9
00660136	Stevie Ray Vaughan – In Step....................$18.9
00660058	Stevie Ray Vaughan – Lightnin' Blues 1983 – 1987....................$22.9
00694835	Stevie Ray Vaughan – The Sky Is Crying ...$18.9
00694776	Vaughan Brothers – Family Style $18.9
00660196	Vixen – Rev It Up.......................................$18.9
00694781	Warrant – Cherry Pie $18.9
00694787	Warrant – Dirty Rotten Filthy Stinking Rich..$18.9
00694866	Warrant – Dog Eat Dog $18.9
00694789	The Muddy Waters Guitar Collection $19.9
00694888	Windham Hill Guitar Sampler.....................$16.9
00694786	Winger $18.9
00694782	Winger – In The Heart Of The Young $18.9
00694900	Winger – Pull...$18.9